A Gift For:

From:

Published in 2013 by Hallmark Gift Books,
a division of Hallmark Cards, Inc.,
Kansas City, MO 64141
Visit us on the Web at Hallmark.com.

Scripture quotations are from the King James
Version of the Bible.

Editorial Director: Delia Berrigan
Editor: Nate Barbarick
Art Director: Chris Opheim
Designer: Scott Swanson
Production Designer: Dan Horton

ISBN: 978-1-59530-961-7
BOK1279

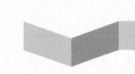

Printed and bound in China

THE PASTOR IS IN

A Thirty-Day Faith Devotional Inspired by Peanuts

Written by Rigel J. Dawson, Minister, and featuring the comic strips of Charles M. Schulz

1. Stick to Your Dreams

2. Charge Goliaths Head-On

3. Let Grief Do Its Good—Then Let Go

4. Slow Down, Charlie Brown

5. Shake Out the Blanket and Move On

6. Watch Your Tongue

7. Reject Your Fears

8. Answer Softly

9. Cast Just a Glance at Riches

10. Appreciate the People Who Matter

11. Admit It When You've Been a Blockhead

12. Thank God for Everything

13. Listen to Your Tone

14. Let Your Loved Ones Off the Hook

15. Minimize What Troubles You

16. Change Your Point of View

17. Admit Your Mistakes

18. Psychiatric Help 5¢

19. Service Is About Others

20. Say Thanks for Salvation

21. Start Counting

22. Don't Just Pray—Strive!

23. Serve Instead of Waiting To Be Served

24. Prepare for Hills and Valleys

25. Put Your Anger Where It Belongs

26. Don't Wait, Act Now

27. Quit Kidding Yourself

28. Keep Your Faith

29. Listen Closely to Criticism

30. Recognize and Prepare for the End

Introduction

This is a labor of love. The words of the psalmist are also my own: *"I love your law!"* God's word is amazing. It comforts me, inspires me, and motivates me. It convicts me, and it corrects me. I stand in awe of its perfection. I am both humbled and astounded by the fact that God is speaking to me through the Bible's pages. To *me*!!! It is one of the great joys of my life to be able to preach and teach the sacred scriptures and to share with others what I have learned from the wonderful words of life.

And how I love *Peanuts*! It is, in my humble opinion, the greatest comic strip ever crafted. There is no word more fitting for Charles M. Schulz's ability than "genius." The little world he created, the wonderful characters he drew, and the wise and witty words he put into their mouths made for a masterpiece. It demonstrates a great sense of humor, usually hilarious, but sometimes soberingly profound. So many of the thousands of daily strips Mr. Schulz drew are little mirrors reflecting our human nature back to us: our joys, our insecurities, our faults and foibles.

I suppose that part of the reason I love *Peanuts* so much is that its creator infused it with spiritual wisdom. This book represents my meager attempt to meld these two great passions of mine. It enables me to share the encouragement of God's word while riding the coattails of Schulz's greatness. I hope that you will have a laugh at the expense of Charlie Brown, Snoopy, Linus, Lucy, and the gang, and that you will be inspired and encouraged by the many timeless teachings of the Bible. Enjoy and be blessed!

Rigel J. Dawson

1

Stick to Your Dreams

It's best to nurture fragile dreams in private until they're strong enough to stand out in the open.

Stick to Your Dreams

You really have to be careful in whom you confide. Dreams are the hints God whispers in your ear about who you really are. They are precious. In fact, they are priceless. And so dreams must be guarded against thieves who would steal them away and leave you without hope.

Many make the mistake of revealing their aspirations to someone who isn't worthy of something so delicate and valuable. Certain people will shatter your dreams with their clumsy comments. They are blind to the value of your personal ambitions, and sometimes it's best to nurture those fragile dreams in private until they're strong enough to stand out in the open.

Then there are the "haters," dissatisfied with their own circumstances, yet unmotivated to work toward change. That's why they scoff at the mere suggestion that you want to grow into something more than you are. Misery loves company, and apathy is always self-conscious in the presence of action. You've heard their lines before: *What makes you think you can do that? Didn't you try that once before? Who do you think you are?* And the really cruel ones just laugh right in your face!

Sadly, these people are sometimes the ones closest to us. I once counseled a young lady who wanted desperately to go back to school but wouldn't do it because her mother kept ridiculing the idea. Wanting to make her mom happy, she deferred her dreams for years until she realized that her mother was really scared of her daughter becoming more independent and no longer needing her. This was nothing more than that mother's selfish desire to maintain the status quo, and it stifled this young woman's aspirations for a long time. Even our most intimate relations are not always the best custodians of our dreams.

What have you set your mind to achieve? What new endeavor have you wanted to attempt? What has your spirit been spurring you to do? *Now, why haven't you made your move yet?* If it's because someone has hijacked your hope, it's time to reclaim what's rightfully yours. First and foremost, reaffirm your faith in yourself—you were made for great things! Then start using the wisdom of discernment to tell the difference between the people who will handle your dream with care and those who will fumble the fragile and precious gifts you have been given.

2

Charge Goliaths Head-On

It takes courage to confront the challenges of life.

Charge Goliaths Head-On

Most of us have witnessed firsthand the failure of this particular philosophy. Sure, this strategy works for a while, but sooner or later, you're forced to face the reality that the problem is still there . . . and likely worse than ever!

Problems are like Michael Myers and Jason Voorhees. Remember those old horror movie villains? One thing that makes those films so frightening is the fact that no matter how fast and furiously the victim-to-be runs away, the villain is always only a few steps behind . . . and he's *WALKING!!!* And just when the prey thinks that they've escaped and can breathe a sigh of relief, they turn around . . . only to be *face-to-face with the killer!*

You can probably recall a similar experience with some troubling situation in your life. It's possible you procrastinated in making necessary decisions or put off tackling hard chores or just ignored an important matter altogether. Maybe you indefinitely tabled a difficult discussion with a family member or friend or put some distressing mail out of sight and out of mind. And all was well for a while . . . until one day, the problem was back, bigger than ever, and staring you right in the face!

It takes courage to confront the challenges of life. The well-known story of David and Goliath is an inspiring example. We can let the giants in our lives continue to intimidate us and back us down day after day, or we can say, "Enough is enough!" and charge them head-on. When we find that kind of strength within ourselves, the surprising result is often a much easier victory than we had anticipated. David had five stones in his bag, but he only needed one!

Is there something you've been trying to run away from? If you're not an avoider, that's great; keep charging your giants! However, if you find in yourself the tendency to delay doing what needs to be done, start praying for a spirit of bravery and boldness. We are called to be conquerors, not cowards. Resolve to stop running; *it's time to stand and fight!*

3

Let Grief Do Its Good–Then Let Go

We should be helping each other carry our burdens, not making them heavier.

Let Grief Do Its Good—Then Let Go

A spirit in need of forgiveness is a fragile thing. Your words and deeds can either lighten the load of guilt that a person is carrying or pile onto the already difficult burden he or she has to bear. Why do we feel the need to make sure people know where they went wrong, even after they've admitted it? What is it within our human nature that compels us to say, *"I told you so!"* or to take it upon ourselves to see that others suffer sufficiently for their mistakes?

We should be helping each other carry our burdens, not making them heavier. Most people know when they've messed up. When their faults and failings lie exposed to the world, what's needed in those critical moments is the grace to comfort them and the love to cover their mistakes. Let me caution you not to confuse love with the liberalism of tolerance. If a person's behavior needs to be corrected, love *demands* that you speak the truth and do all that you can to turn them back to the right path. Those whom we fail to rebuke when they're wrong, we really don't love at all **(Hebrews 12:6)**. However, once people admit their mistakes, love substitutes the slap in the face with a pat on the back.

Shame and regret can be destructive forces. Guilt can consume a person. That's why we must be careful not to compound its *negative* effects once it has worked its *positive* purpose of provoking a change.

Do you feel the need to reinforce the guilty feelings of others when they fall short? Do you find it hard to resist the urge to elaborate on their errors?

If we honestly examine what we say and do, we'll all discover our guilt in this regard to some degree. Purge your spirit of the impulse to put your foot on the necks of those who have fallen down. Consider the damage you're doing when you assume the role of "punisher." Not only are you adding to the emotional weight they have to endure, but you're probably eroding your relationships with them in the process. You may be planting the seeds of bitterness, which will eventually bear the fruits of anger and alienation. Once grief has done its good, help the people you love to let it go . . . you may need *their* help before too long!

4

Slow Down, Charlie Brown

Don't let the rapid pace of society make you miss what's really important.

Slow Down, Charlie Brown

We have become addicted to activity. The effect of our amped-up, achievement-driven culture is that many of us have become slaves to our vocations—and even slaves to our *vacations!*

We work harder and harder. We fill every waking moment with some labor intended to get us ahead or, at the very least, to keep us on pace with the pack. This mentality seeps into our recreation. We can hardly relax anymore for competing and pushing ourselves to be "extreme." Just look at the average cruise itinerary; it's loaded with jet skiing, sightseeing, shopping, golfing, snorkeling, rock climbing, parasailing, and every kind of adventure!

The wise king Solomon was addicted to accomplishment until he realized the pointlessness of his pursuits:

- Those yet to come won't even remember what you achieved.
- Someone else will inherit everything that you've earned . . . and that person may be a wasteful fool who squanders in no time what it took you a lifetime to build.

• No matter what you do, you are still destined for the dust.

Now let's be clear: there's nothing wrong with being driven . . . as long as you request frequent stops along the way! Don't let the rapid pace of society cause you to miss what's really important. Don't neglect to nurture your marriage. Don't overlook the lives of your children. Don't fail to savor your friendships. And above all, don't forget to feed your spirit!

We've bought wholeheartedly into the "Just do it!" mentality, but we need to modify that mantra and start telling ourselves to "Just *be* it!" What we desperately need is a radical redefinition of "success."

Pray today for a renewed spirit, and the ability to see success for yourself and your family not in terms of doing what the world dictates, but in terms of being what you're called to be. Just be a good, attentive father. Just be a sensitive and caring mother. Just be a loyal and loving friend . . . a faithful, considerate husband . . . a devoted and diligent wife. Just *be* it!

5

Shake Out the Blanket and Move On

How much harder do we make it for ourselves when we keep holding on to yesterday?

Shake Out the Blanket and Move On

Have you mastered the art of forgetfulness? I'm not talking about the natural tendency that comes with age, but the *skill* that comes through *practice*. If not, you need to. One of the biggest obstacles to our success is that we insist on carrying baggage that should have been dropped off long ago. The Apostle Paul provides us with a powerful example. He writes in **Philippians 3:13**, "but this one thing I do, forgetting those things which are behind."

Many of us are holding on to the hurts of the past, refusing to forgive those who have wronged us. Others have immortalized their own failures and worn them like so many charms on a bracelet as daily reminders of their faults and flaws.

It is already a struggle living for today and straining toward tomorrow. How much harder do we make it for ourselves when we keep holding on to yesterday?!? Some things that are behind us have to be abandoned in order to attain what's ahead. If the soil of your spirit is so bitter, where will the seeds of positive ideas and rewarding relationships grow and bear fruit? If you expend all of your energy beating up on yourself for past shortcomings, how will you have the strength to fight off the insults and discouragement of the next naysayer when he inevitably comes along?

We tend to blame everything and everyone else for hindering our progress, but often we are the ones who refuse to let go of the old in order to grasp the new. Search your heart today for any "leftovers" that need to be thrown away. Is there a record of wrongs you've been keeping—either against yourself or someone else—that needs to be wiped clean? It's time to forgive yourself and step out of that prison of your own design. It's time to release the hurts and the hard feelings that you've been harboring toward others. It's time to shake out the blanket and move on.

6

Watch Your Tongue

It is of utmost importance that we learn to listen.

Watch Your Tongue

Most of us, at some point in time, have spoken too soon. We have interjected our uninformed opinions before getting all the facts. Or we have responded too rapidly to someone's statements without really understanding what was intended. The results of chiming in prematurely can range from mild embarrassment to utter disaster. Doing so has wrecked relationships, cost people their jobs, instigated costly conflicts, and led to deep public humiliation!

James 1:19 urges us to be quick to listen and slow to speak, but we often do just the opposite. The reasons for our haste in speaking are many. Pride makes us think more highly of our opinions than we should. Anger often causes us to cut others off. And sometimes when we speak too soon, we do so out of pure motives; we really do have truth to share and something positive to contribute, but we're so anxious to offer it that we rudely silence someone else.

It is of utmost importance that we learn to listen. Even if we don't *verbally* interject, many of us have the habit of *mentally* cutting other people off while they're still talking. We're busy readying our responses rather than receiving what's being said. This is not fair to those whom we claim to love.

Love is patient. It should provoke you to pump the brakes on your responses and allow those in your life to communicate openly and honestly without fear of being run over. It should make you mindful to search for the meaning in what others are saying and to seek understanding before you reply. And it should cause you to consider whether or not you need to reply at all. Not everything a person expresses to you is an invitation for your opinion. Sometimes, the people in your life just need to be heard.

From this day forward, resolve to work on tuning in to what others are saying, especially those closest to you. Make up your mind to stop being so impulsive in your speech and apologize to your loved ones who have been hurt by your impetuous and impudent interruptions. Rein in your runaway words . . . *before you have to eat them!*

7

Reject Your Fears

Apprehension and anxiety are not the attitudes God has given us.

Reject Your Fears

We've been told that there's nothing to fear but fear itself. But most of us remain a little skeptical of that assertion. It seems there's *plenty* to be afraid of. Thoughts of harm befalling the children plague our minds. The specters of injury and disease loom large at times. And news of terrorism, robberies, and assaults condition us to constantly look over our shoulders.

And then there is the future! We fear losing loved ones, losing jobs and homes, losing financial security, and even losing our very minds to the stresses of everyday life. There is plenty to fear but no good reason for the child of God to fear it!

Apprehension and anxiety are *not* the attitudes God has given to us; those are carried over from the animal fight or flight responses. Faith in God gives us a new spirit: one of power, love, and self-discipline.

And remember, God *is* love. **I John 4:18** says, "There is no fear in love; but perfect love casteth out fear." Most fear is irrational; therefore, when the love of God drives it away, we are left with clear minds. Even though irrational anxieties creep in from time to time, meditation on the Spirit brings us back to sanity, reminding us that most of what we fear will never come to pass anyway. And even if it does, God is still strong enough to deliver us from it!

Take a few moments of meditation right now to consider the fears that you regularly entertain. What are you worried about? Collect these anxieties. In fact, write them down and read them over. Be honest and be specific. Go ahead, I'll wait . . .

Good. *Now rebuke them and reject them as unreal to your renewed spirit!* Refuse to allow them to oppress your mind for one more day. Take whatever reasonable precautions against them that you can, but then resolve to simply trust in the Lord and be at ease. Find in your daily prayers the strength to drive away those fears and replace them with peace.

8

Answer Softly

When you turn the other cheek, most people will apologize.

Answer Softly

The next time someone attacks you, try disarming that person instead of fighting back. When you respond with a "soft answer" **(Proverbs 15:1)**, your gentleness makes it very difficult for your attacker to sustain the assault. Tenderness has an almost miraculous way of turning aside aggression. Anyone with a reasonable amount of human decency and compassion *must* stop swinging when the opponent refuses to fight.

The driving force behind most of the personal assaults you will experience is anger. Anger is a powerful emotion, and when unchecked by love and self-control, it causes people to speak and act abusively to those around them. However, when you find yourself on the receiving end of wrath, and you say or do something to defuse the assailant's anger, it's just like taking their weapons away. Think about that; you probably know from personal experience how hard it is to criticize an especially kind person or to show hostility in the face of another's humility.

Now admittedly, this is no easy task. The natural reaction to being struck a blow is to pay it back in kind. But the *super*natural reaction is to repay good for evil and to show meekness when met with enmity. When you humbly and patiently offer the other cheek after a blow's been struck, most people will not only *not* strike the second blow, but they will likely apologize for the first one.

   Once you take their weapons away, most people will forsake the fight and be ashamed by their behavior. Pray for a stronger spirit of self-discipline, one that will empower you to refrain from retaliating. Use some wisdom to find the right response for the situation. Start practicing the spiritual art of disarming the enemy by taking his anger away.

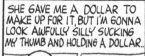

Cast Just a Glance at Riches

Real security is in a rewarding relationship with the giver of every gift, not in the gift itself.

Cast Just a Glance at Riches

Many of us fall into the trap of thinking that the more money we have, the better life will be. We buy the lie that it will soothe the stress in our marriages and homes. The kids' attitudes wouldn't be so disgruntled; we could move to a better neighborhood, one without so much trouble and temptation; I would finally have the time to live my dreams and be freed to become the person I know I can be.

Yeah . . . *right*.

Money will never give you true security because, by its very nature, money is *insecure*. The wise man warns that "riches certainly make themselves wings; they fly away as an eagle toward heaven" **(Proverbs 23:5)**. Money attracts "friends" by the dozens who are more than happy to help you put it to good use. An emergency can exhaust abundant savings in a matter of weeks. Swindlers are always scheming, and thieves are ever lying in wait. Investments can go bad and economies can collapse overnight. That's why we are urged to show the wisdom of restraint and not wear ourselves out to become rich with things that do not last **(v. 4)**.

What we need to do is to live beyond our means. No, I'm not suggesting that we all go crazy with credit and dig a hole of debt. I'm saying that we should live *above* mere material things and learn to stop looking to "stuff" for a sense of security it can never supply. Real security is in a rewarding relationship with the *giver* of every gift, not in the gift itself. It is in having hope that no one can heist, finding peace that can't be plucked from your grasp, and gaining a sense of satisfaction that circumstance can't snatch away.

Take a few moments of meditation to carefully examine your relationship to money. Be honest with yourself. Is your desire for material things forcing you to forfeit time with loved ones? Are you falling behind spiritually in order to "get ahead" materially? Has your love of money become the root of some evil in your life?

Pray to be purged of the spirit of materialism and to renew your mindset on money. Recommit yourself to seeking *true* security in the things that no moth can destroy, no rust can corrupt, and no thief can steal.

10

Appreciate the People Who Matter

A few well-spoken words of admiration can energize you to do even more than you thought was possible!

Appreciate the People Who Matter

Everyone needs validation. The human spirit, just like the engine of a car, will sputter and die without the proper maintenance. Lack of esteem, especially from those whose opinions we respect, can lead to dejection and defeat. Not that we should ever strive solely for the praise of others, but we must acknowledge the positive impact that praise can have on our spirits. A few well-spoken words of admiration can energize you to do even more than you thought was possible!

Think about the people whose contributions to your life you value the most. Maybe your parents did a masterful job of placing you on the proper path in life. Maybe a sibling picked you up more times than you can count. Perhaps a special teacher inspired you, or a trusted counselor steered you from disaster. Maybe a friend of yours is the epitome of what a friend should be. Or maybe there is a spiritual leader who has been a profound example to you and your family. Do they know how you feel about who they are and what they have done?

Here's an assignment for you. Make a list of three important people in your life, people who have made a positive impact. Sometime over the course of the next three days, talk to them and let them know that they are appreciated . . . *and let them know why!* If you live with the person, take a few minutes to sit down face to face and share your appreciation. A few simple, sincere words can validate this loved one's presence and purpose in your life. If you feel something urging you to get back in touch with someone who's meant a lot to you, don't resist it—your words may be just what that person needs to lift his or her spirits in a time of depression or doubt.

One of the first verses of scripture I ever committed to memory was **Proverbs 25:11**. It says, "A word fitly spoken is like apples of gold in pictures of silver."

The right word at the right time is indeed a beautiful and precious thing. Don't neglect the potential of your positive words to strengthen the spirits of your loved ones and fire them up to keep fighting the good fight. You have the power . . . use it!

11

Admit It When You've Been a Blockhead

Stop griping about how unfair everything is—it's time to own it.

Admit It When You've Been a Blockhead

'Fessing up is hard to do, but sometimes it's the only thing that will turn your situation around. Note the teaching of David in **Psalm 32:3-5**: When we keep silent our guilt eats away at us. But when we confess, we are forgiven and our hearts are made light.

To "confess" is literally to "speak the same thing" as someone else, to agree with what another has said. In regard to our sin, confession is agreeing with God that it was wrong. He has spoken to us about good and evil, right and wrong. He has told us what He approves and disapproves. Therefore, when we are wrong, we must not try to rationalize or justify it; we must simply submit to the truth and *agree* with God.

Acknowledgment of our sin also includes acknowledgment of the consequences. In other words, you may have some tough pills to swallow to heal your heart and spirit. Continuing to act as though you don't deserve what's happening is, in essence, to say a just and righteous God is acting with injustice and unrighteousness.

What sin lingers in your life? What have you been doing or saying that goes against the will of your God? And what consequences have you been dealing with as a result of that? Stop making excuses for yourself. Stop groaning and griping about how unfair everything is—it's time to own it. After all, it's yours. Wrongdoing has its consequences; however, complete and candid confession opens the door for forgiveness and for your freedom from the consequences of sin. God will cleanse you when you come clean, and He will restore the joy of your salvation **(Psalm 51:7-12)**. What will it take for you to 'fess up to your faults?

EMPTY! AND I'M DYING OF THIRST!

5-19

Thank God for Everything

The magnificence of God's heavens is almost too much to fathom.

Thank God for Everything

David's mind was blown, too, when he thought about the goodness of a great and awesome God toward small and insignificant humans. He asked, "What is man, that thou art mindful of him?" **(Psalm 8:4)**. When you consider the size and scope of God's heavens and the magnificence of the moon and stars He has hung in the universe, it is almost too much to fathom that a majestic God can still attend to such lowly things as us! The soul-stirring, jaw-dropping, mind-blowing reality is that, of all creation, man is the Creator's pride and joy.

Today, think about a time in your life when you couldn't see a way out of your puzzling predicament . . . *and then God made a way out of no way!* Think about a time when you had done all you could possibly do, and it still wasn't enough . . . *and then God stepped in to accomplish what you couldn't!* Think about a time when your ability was inadequate and your intelligence was insufficient, a time when your limitations loomed in front of you like an uncrossable chasm . . . *and then God built a bridge out of the thin blue air!* Think about a time when you were deep in a ditch of your own design . . . *and then God reached down to deliver you when you didn't even deserve to be delivered!*

Say a special prayer of thanksgiving for all those times in your life. See as Abraham did: the Lord will provide **(Genesis 22:14)**. Thank Him with a joyful heart for the ram in the bush, the rain right on time, and the supply for your every need. The great God of the universe still sits high and looks low—think about *that* for a while.

13

Listen to Your Tone

Words can be weapons, and we must be careful how we wield them.

Listen to Your Tone

We know how the old "sticks and stones" tune goes, but the truth of the matter is that words *do* hurt. They can hurt a lot. Words can bruise feelings, stir up wrath, and break spirits. The wrong word at the wrong time can utterly humiliate a person. One injurious utterance can start a firm friendship on a slow decline toward disintegration, or even destroy it instantaneously. Families have been fractured by nothing more than a simple sentence. A few well-placed words from a spiteful naysayer can kill inspiration, smother enthusiasm, and demolish dreams. Words can be weapons, and we must be careful how we wield them.

Many of us don't even realize the negative effects that some of our words have on others, especially those closest to us. Start watching your words more closely from now on, particularly in the context of your intimate relationships. Unfortunately, it is with these people that we grow comfortable, and it is on them that we tend to take out our daily angers and annoyances through the words that we speak.

- Do you habitually attach a "yeah, *but*" to every good suggestion that's made?

- Do you regularly use sarcastic, snippy, or snide responses?
- Do you point out flaws and failings even when it's not necessary or constructive to do so?
- Do you compare your spouse or child or friend unfavorably to other people?
- Do you hurl insults when you're angry or resort to name-calling when you're frustrated?
- Do you constantly bring up past transgressions and make others repeatedly relive their failures?

If so, then your words may be kindling a fire in someone's spirit. Such a fire, stoked up by the words you speak, may eventually consume your loved one from within, and it may even begin the blaze that burns down the relationship you've built!

Open your ears and start listening to the true tone and tenor of your words. Study your speech more closely from now on and see whether what you say serves to build others up or burn them down. Humbly ask for forgiveness if you find hurtful words on your lips, and then start to cultivate a pure heart, from which pure words will flow.

Let Your Loved Ones Off the Hook

We should be a whole person, in and of ourselves.

Let Your Loved Ones Off the Hook

We often hold other people to a standard that's *way* too high. Many have assigned the significant others in their lives the impossible task of making them happy. Given the immensity of the endeavor, no wonder they're disappointed time and time again. The very notion that another person can give you what he or she doesn't even possess is ridiculous. Your friends are still seeking fulfillment of their own; *how are they going to offer you what they have yet to find for themselves?* Your spouse is searching for satisfaction just like you are; *how is he or she going to give it to you?*

Many have abandoned relationships that had incredible potential because they were trying to get from someone else what he or she did not even have to give! *"He didn't make me feel like I hoped he would." "She didn't make me happy." "I didn't feel fulfilled when we were together."* And so they ended up forfeiting what could have been a beautiful thing. Many of us are waiting for the "Jerry Maguire moment," that instant when we encounter the person to whom we can say, "You complete me." But other people aren't in your life to *complete* you; they're there to *complement* you. You should be a whole person, in and of yourself, having a fully-developed identity that's defined by your own deeply-felt sense of personal purpose. Positive relationships that provide strength and joy are just the icing; knowing and loving yourself is the cake!

No one else has what you're looking for; they're all looking for it too! Determine today to let the loved ones in your life off the hook for your happiness, and resolve to appreciate the blessings they bring your way just by being who they are. No one else can give you happiness; you've got to make up your own mind to have it, regardless of who comes or goes.

Minimize What Troubles You

Every new thing we get is another new thing to care for, protect, and maintain.

Minimize What Troubles You

There are countless concerns vying for your attention and competing for a spot on your list of worries. There seems to be an ever-expanding inventory of new threats, new shortages, new cutbacks, new health concerns, and the list goes on. Over much of the world around us we have little or no control, and it's only natural to be concerned with the way things are going. What's unnatural and unnecessary is to compound your sense of unease with complications of your own creation!

For one thing, the accumulation of material things encumbers us with anxieties our ancestors never had. Every new thing we get is another new thing to care for, protect, and maintain. And it's another new thing to accessorize with even *more* new things. There's nothing wrong with having nice possessions, but you should be enjoying them, not stressing over them. Is there some big, beautiful bauble in your life that's become more of a burden than a blessing? Is there something you need to cut loose for the sake of your sanity and your spirituality? Although our modern society wouldn't agree, simplicity is an admirable aspiration.

Then there are the worries that we manufacture out of thin air. Many live daily under the crushing weight of things that don't even exist! They constantly worry over *what if?* "What if I lose my job?" "What if I get a serious illness?" "What if . . . what if . . . what if?" Well, what if none of those things come to pass? Tomorrow isn't even here yet, and we could reduce our anxieties by 99.9 percent if we just worried one day at a time! Snoopy knew this secret.

Today, take some time to examine those anxious areas of your life and make up your mind to minimize your worries. Take a good, long look at your personal list of anxieties; figure out which things are just not worth your worry, and pray for the power to let them go.

Change Your Point of View

*Count your blessings, and when you're done,
start counting all over again.*

Change Your Point of View

Everything depends on your perspective. You can choose to lament your limitations and mourn your mistakes, or you can turn your attention to the abilities you *do* possess and the opportunity each new day provides to fix your faults and failures. You can expend your mental energy anticipating the terrors of tomorrow, or you can determine that you will bask in the blessings of today.

You have to discipline your spirit to concentrate on the good stuff. The Apostle Paul urges us to think on things that are true, noble, right, and pure; things that are lovely, admirable, excellent, and praiseworthy **(Philippians 4:8)**. The word "think" in that passage literally means "to make an account of" or "to calculate" something. This means that you have to train your brain to constantly count and add up the positive things you experience. Count your blessings, and when you're done, *start counting all over again.* Do it until the practice becomes your habit, and the habit becomes your character. Soon it will be second nature for you to see the good in every situation and to stay in the mental state of contentment.

And be careful of those who rain on your rejoicing parade and think they're doing you the favor of "bringing you back to reality." Some people seem to have made it their mission in life to make sure everyone around them stays "grounded" on their same level of discouragement and defeat. But don't ever allow anyone to pull you down when your spirit is soaring high.

You're only hurting yourself when you look forward to the next problem. Those who fail to celebrate the blessings of the here-and-now become disgruntled and bitter because they expend all their emotional energy anticipating hardships just over the horizon. Instead of fixating on what may go wrong, we should rejoice over what's right *right now*.

If your head has been hanging low, resolve to stop rehearsing the negative and start reveling in the positive. Aspire to a new frame of mind, and shift your perspective from what *isn't* to what *is*. If school's out, quit wasting your summer dreading the fall!

Admit Your Mistakes

Blame really doesn't solve anything.

Admit Your Mistakes

Man has been playing the blame game since the beginning of time. When he was called to account, the first words out of Adam's mouth were, *"It was all that woman's fault!"* Then when it was Eve's turn, we heard the very first declaration of a refrain that's been echoing ever since: *"The devil made me do it!"* Man seems to have a genetically-encoded propensity to pass the buck!

Blame really *doesn't* solve anything. It's a pretty good pacifier to quiet your conscience, but it's ultimately ineffective. Regardless of to whom you try to assign the guilt, if you were involved, you are still accountable. Why haven't we learned that lesson yet? When you tried to justify your bad behavior as a child by telling what a brother or sister did first to "make" you do what you did, you still got punished! Maybe your sibling was disciplined too, but blaming him or her didn't take you off the hook. Telling your parent that you weren't the one who started it or that all of your friends were doing it too did nothing to remove your personal responsibility in the matter.

On top of that, blame stunts personal growth. As long as you keep evading responsibility and shifting blame for your shortcomings to others, you remain in a state of spiritual infancy. The more accustomed you become to assigning your guilt to someone else, the easier it gets for you to persist in your wrongdoing. When everything is always someone else's fault, your conscience gradually loses power. Sincere confession doesn't say, "I did it, *but* . . . " Sincere confession that truly sets you free to move forward simply says, "I did it." This is a sure sign of maturity.

Is there something in your life that's still dogging your steps because you've tried to assign the guilt to someone else rather than owning what's yours? Are you hurting an important relationship by stubbornly standing your ground of denial and blame? Are you spiritually stagnant because you refuse to grow up and admit your faults? It might make you feel better, but playing the blame game always ends in a loss.

18

Psychiatric Help 5¢

*Be receptive to the blessings that come
from the wisdom of the wise.*

Psychiatric Help 5¢

The wise man teaches us that without good advice, our plans will disappoint; only after seeking counsel may we establish our purpose **(Proverbs 15:22)**. You should never set out on any significant undertaking without seeking the insight of prudent people. There are many in your life who have been there and done that. They can offer assistance and support. They can warn you of the pitfalls along the path and help you anticipate your enemies' attacks. You should always be receptive to the blessings that come from the wisdom of the wise.

Open-mindedness, however, must be tempered by the ability to appraise the value of the advice. There will never be a shortage of people who want to play the role of adviser in your life. However, not everyone has advice worth heeding, and not everyone has your best interests at heart. Many people are living confused and chaotic lives due to the foolish counselors who influence them.

Some people have never pitched a game in their lives. Why in the world would you listen to them when you're on the mound? Evaluate the experience level of a person before you accept his or her word as gospel. If this person hasn't even attempted to do what you're trying to accomplish, let alone done it *successfully*, it is probably best to take that information with a grain of salt and seek a second opinion. Many a good marriage has been ruined by bad advice from a single friend who couldn't even sustain a steady relationship!

You also need to recognize the motives and the moods of those who counsel you. Some only want to control you and move you in the direction that suits their purposes. Others offer advice out of their own anger and discontentment, hoping to use you as the tool for their aggression. Still others would like nothing more than to see you fall flat on your face. Keep your eyes and ears open to the intentions of your would-be advisers.

Pray for clarity and focus. Ask yourself what *you* want to do. Then find people of intelligence and integrity on whom you can rely for additional guidance. Learn to discern, and find the strength to say, "thanks, but no thanks" to those "coaches" who don't know a slider from a fast ball.

Service Is About Others

Search your spirit for any pride that needs to be tempered.

Service Is About Others

Some are just in it for the glamour and the glory. Sure, they talk the talk of humility and cooperation, but when they have to walk the walk, they stumble. Just for the record, how many fly balls has Lucy dropped over the years?

We all have excuses. *If it doesn't come with a spotlight, count me out! If it doesn't involve the possibility of a promotion, I don't have the time! If I won't be publicly acknowledged at the end, find someone else!* Every believer needs to be reminded now and again of what it means to be a Christian: it is a life of *service!* The sad reality is that much of what God calls us to do we consider unworthy of our effort. Jesus reminds His disciples that the servant is not greater than his master **(John 15:20)**. Paul urges us to have the same attitude Christ had: He took on the life of a servant, humbled Himself, and became obedient even to the point of dying on the cross **(Philippians 2:6-8)**. Surely *we* can muster up a little more meekness!

Consoling the sick and comforting the diseased and dying. Feeding the hungry and clothing the naked. Setting up before and cleaning up afterwards. Arriving early and staying late. Ministering to those who are considered "difficult," those with whom most would rather not even associate. These are tasks we often shun because of pride. However, in **I Corinthians 12:15-16**, Paul reminds us that no one can say, "Because I am not the hand, I am not of the body." You may not be called to the prominent position or be given the glorious task, but you are still ordained for a unique function in the world. In verse **22**, the apostle affirms that the weaker parts of the body are actually *indispensable* to its effective functioning.

Don't be like Lucy and think more highly of yourself than you should. God gives grace to the humble. Search your spirit for any pride that needs to be tempered. Reacquaint yourself with humility, and resolve to emulate Jesus' example more faithfully from now on.

Say Thanks for Salvation

*If you walk daily in the joy of your salvation,
it will be obvious to everyone.*

Say Thanks for Salvation

Have you forgotten what it feels like to be taken off the hook? If so, think back. I know this is an uncomfortable exercise, but it's necessary to reclaim the joy of your salvation. Just for a moment, crack open the closet and look at all the skeletons there: your most loathsome deeds, your most venomous words, the worst things you have ever done.

Okay, you can shut the closet door now. Sorry to put you through that, but just think, whatever you were once guilty of—from the littlest white lie to the most grievous iniquity—*God has let you off the hook!*

Believers in God have been forgiven! We have been declared "NOT GUILTY" of all charges! Of all people, our laughter should be the loudest!

Any saved sinner who isn't rejoicing probably needs a memory refresher. Once you forget that you've been forgiven, you will soon be living like your old sinful self. Peter calls this a spiritual near-sightedness that leads to an unfruitful life without joy, goodness, brotherly kindness, or love

(II Peter 1:5-9). If, however, you walk daily in the joy of your salvation, it will be obvious to those who witness your walk with Jesus. Say a special prayer of thanksgiving today.

Pour out your gratitude for everything you have. Ask Him to revive the spirit of joy within you if your enthusiasm has waned. If you have been suppressing that spirit for the sake of appearances, pray for the courage to forget about what others think and let loose with jubilant exultation. God has done marvelous things, and He is worthy to be praised in the sight of all people.

Start Counting

Living mindfully of your mortality can lead to a more joyful life.

Start Counting

David cried out to the Lord to make him mindful of the measure of his life. He said, "Lord, make me to know mine end, and the measure of my days, what it is: that I may know how frail I am" **(Psalm 39:4)**. Although it is a sobering exercise, remembering your mortality is an important one. Time is a gift, but it is one we often take for granted. Every now and then you need to check the clock.

Not that any of us can know exactly how much time we have left, but the point is to understand that time is limited. We settle so comfortably into the flow of life that we lose sight of the fact that time is running out, and we stop living with a sense of spiritual urgency. Diligent prayer and study take a back seat to our daily duties and deadlines. Quality time with the family is postponed. Service is delayed indefinitely and benevolence is deferred. Paul tells us to walk very carefully, not as fools, but with wisdom. We are to seize opportunity, because the days are evil **(Ephesians 5:15-16)**.

Remembering your mortality can be a jarring thing, but it need not be depressing or distressing. In fact, living mindfully of your mortality can lead to a more joyful life, one lived in constant appreciation of every moment. It can motivate you to do away with some of the non-essential stuff in your world and give you a simpler and more satisfying life.

Thank the Lord today for your life, and truly express your gratitude for every day above ground. Pause to contemplate the fragility of your existence and the fleeting nature of your humanity. Pray for focus to start attending to the really important things that He has called you to accomplish with the time you've been granted.

And after you've prayed, make it a point to set some spiritual goals for yourself. Decide what you need to accomplish for the Lord within the next month, the next six months, the next year. The clock is ticking. You are 147 seconds older now than when you started reading this . . .

Don't Just Pray—Strive!

We have to take responsibility for our own happiness.

Don't Just Pray—Strive!

If only it were that easy! Good days aren't free, and they don't come simply by request. Even as we pray for peace, we must never forget that God will answer those prayers in different ways. One thing the Bible reveals is that we must not only *ask* for good and pleasant days, but we must *act* in order to make them a reality.

This is the part where many of us tune out. We have no problem praying for God's blessings, but we tend to overlook the fact that many of those blessings depend on what we do. We have to take responsibility for our own happiness. We must turn away from evil and seek peace **(I Peter 3:10-11)**. If you truly desire good days, you must live your life so as to bring them about.

There's no way around this one; if you want peace and prosperity, you must do good things! You can't be a world-class "fussbudget" like Lucy and expect to find happiness and serenity.

We are encouraged to be *pursuers* of peace. Peace can be elusive, so effort is essential. You must become active in hunting it down, going the extra mile to get it, and struggling to maintain it once it's found. This involves the hard work of humility and the labor of loving even the unlovable. This requires biting your tongue, swallowing your pride, and turning the other cheek. It is strenuous work, but well worth every ounce of energy. Don't stop praying for good days, but start to also pray for the strength to strive for them.

Serve Instead of Waiting To Be Served

It's time to release our negative feelings and rediscover the joy of service.

Serve Instead of Waiting To Be Served

A sense of entitlement can be a very dangerous thing. It causes you to get up off of your knees and cease to serve as you should. Do you ever get angry when things don't go your way or when you don't get what you want? Do you ever get a little disgruntled with God and think something like, "I can't believe this is happening to *me*"? After all, you're His child and you've put your faith in Him and tried to live right, haven't you? It's only fair that He gives you what you want, right? **Wrong!** When these feelings rise within you, it's time to check yourself. Nobody owes you anything, least of all God.

Sometimes we forget about grace. Paul reminds believers that we are saved by grace through faith. We are not saved by our own works; therefore, we have no reason whatsoever to boast. Read **Ephesians 2:8-9**. It doesn't matter how many mission trips you've taken or how many homeless shelters or hospitals you've visited. That is all well and good, but you and I are only getting into glory because of the love and goodness of God, and we better not ever start to think otherwise.

All of those things that we have done since being saved amount to nothing more than our "reasonable service" **(Romans 12:1)**. We do them because it just makes sense to serve the God to whom we owe our very souls. The living sacrifices we make don't entitle us to anything; they are the least we can offer God of what *He* is entitled to for paying the awful price of our redemption.

Pray to have a renewed focus on God's grace from this day forward. If you've become embittered because you haven't gotten what you feel entitled to, it's time to release those negative feelings and rediscover the joy of service. Even the Lord Jesus Himself did not come to be served, but to serve. Stop expecting all good all the time and being angry when you don't get it. Start living from this moment with the realization that whatever good you get is more than you deserve.

Prepare for Hills and Valleys

If you never came down, God could never lift you back up!

Prepare for Hills and Valleys

You've got to face the facts: as long as you live in this world, no matter how high you climb, eventually you've got to come back down. There's no avoiding it. You can be living large on one of life's peaks, but sooner or later, you will have to face the valley once again. Yes, it's discouraging, but if you never came down, God could never lift you back up!

Perspective is everything when it comes to running the Christian race. You've got to understand that your life really isn't about you; you were only created to glorify your Creator. Sometimes we lose sight of that fact and fail to realize that our valleys really provide the perfect venue for God to perform His wonderful work. When you are healthy, wealthy, and wise, it is easy for you to become self-sufficient, relying on what you've accumulated and accomplished. But when you're in the valley, there is no choice but to trust in the Lord. When you are strong and stable, it is easy to become lifted up in pride. But when you're in the valley, you *have* to be humble and look to the Lord to lead you out. Remember what He has revealed: "My strength is made perfect in weakness" **(II Corinthians 12:9)**.

If this is an "up" in your life, rejoice in the abundance that God gives. But take this time to grow closer to Him and gird yourself for the next valley. Understand that it's only a matter of time, and ask God to equip you with spiritual stamina so you'll be ready when it comes.

If this is a "down" in your life, don't let it defeat you. Resolve to focus not on the darkness that surrounds you, but on the deliverance of God, which is never far away. He will lift you up again; this too is only a matter of time. Pray for a spirit of submission to His will even while you're in the valley—*especially* while you're in the valley—so that He can accomplish His will, gain His glory, and exalt you in due time!

25

Put Your Anger Where It Belongs

Practice asking yourself, "What am I really mad at?"

Put Your Anger Where It Belongs

Anger has the tendency, when unchecked, to spread from the original object of the emotion to other people and things that had nothing to do with it. Sometimes you bring the hard day home and unleash pent-up aggravations on your family. Sometimes there is one individual who has wronged you, but because you are either unable or unwilling to confront that person, someone else becomes a convenient target for your frustration.

There is also a sort of nebulous anger. Many are mad, but don't really know why. There is a vague bitterness growing in their spirits that they have yet to define and deal with. It becomes increasingly difficult for them to find joy even where it *should* be found. When asked for a reason for their unreasonable actions, they always come up empty.

If that vague variety of anger is corrupting your life with no clear *outward* cause, start to search *within*. If you find you're having trouble pinpointing the roots of your anger, get some help. First, ask God's Spirit to lead you as you devote yourself to study and prayer over the matter. Then talk to a spiritual leader or a mental health professional for guidance. Don't let misplaced anger corrupt the good things God has given you and ruin your ability to enjoy your blessings.

Remember, it is not a sin to experience anger, but what we *do* with it may very well be wicked **(Ephesians 4:26)**. One way to avoid sinning when you become angry is to practice asking yourself, "What am I *really* mad at?" If the answer is not a loved one, make a decision to direct your fury away from them. It is unfair to penalize the people in your life for offenses they have not committed. If this is your habit, you need to kick it quickly!

When anger is provoked by a certain person, you need to find the boldness to confront that individual with love as soon as possible. Pray for wisdom and courage to aim your anger in the right direction and use it as a *constructive* force before it becomes a *destructive* force.

Figure out what you're *really* mad at, and leave everybody else alone!

Don't Wait, Act Now

Many of us are so intimidated by the possibility of failure that we never even try.

Don't Wait, Act Now

What is so special about tomorrow? It will be 24 hours long just like today and yesterday. There is nothing inherently better about it, yet that is the day we schedule all of our appointments with success and all of our dates with destiny. Think for a moment about what God has placed upon your heart to achieve. We all have some goal we want to accomplish. Maybe it's the degree you want to earn or the business you want to open. Maybe it's the song that's been in your head for years that you want to record, or the novel that you're sure would find an audience. Maybe you have been intending to fortify your marriage or strengthen your relationship with your kids. Surely there's some aspiration you have that has been on the shelf for so long that you've forgotten it was even there! Take it down and dust it off. Take a good, long look at that goal and ask yourself why you haven't gone for it.

Are you being lazy? Some of your dreams call for sweat and toil. In order to get where you want to be, you've got to take the long, arduous journey. The wise man confronts us with the question, "How long wilt thou sleep, O sluggard? when wilt thou arise out of thy sleep?" **(Proverbs 6:9)**. Enjoying the ease of today may be *pleasurable*, but it's certainly not *profitable* when it comes to the accomplishment of your goals.

Are you afraid? Many of us are so intimidated by the possibility of failure that we never even try. But I'll take knowing it didn't work out over wondering if it would have any day of the week. Ask God to empower you to overcome the intimidation of imagined things and to embrace the very real and potent power that He provides.

Pray this day for the strength to *move*. Take one step at a time, and do a little every day. Discipline yourself to do it *now*. Don't try to do it all in one day, but don't let another day go by without at least doing something. Tomorrow may never come. Every dream deferred until tomorrow is another regret to toss on the scrapheap of yesterday. Do it today while you have the vision, the ability, and the opportunity that God has graciously given!

Quit Kidding Yourself

People want to be around those who listen, who regard them as significant, and who treat them with respect.

Quit Kidding Yourself

It's easy to fall into the trap of self-deception. We're quick to attribute the negative reactions we receive from other people to problems *they* possess. We rationalize that they must be jealous or resentful of us. We reason to ourselves that they're just mean or that they have some issues. We figure they are just lashing out because of their own insecurities or that they're taking their frustrations out on us. Maybe the truth is not nearly as complicated as that. Maybe you're just not all that likable.

Before you jump to the conclusion that the problem lies with someone else, take the time to search yourself. Examine the way you came across in your interactions. Study the tone of your words, and consider carefully what you said. Were you abrupt or abrasive? Did you minimize or even belittle their ideas? If you are arrogant or overbearing, people will naturally respond negatively toward you. Don't deceive yourself. It's not always other people; sometimes you're just getting the reaction you deserve.

Remember that it's not all about you. Other people have opinions, ideas, and experiences that are equally worth sharing as your own. People gravitate toward those who accept them as equals. They want to be around those who listen, and who regard them as significant and treat them with respect. If you want the fellowship of good friends, you must heed the exhortation to be humble and consider others better than yourself **(Philippians 2:3)**.

Many people are spiritually stagnant in terms of personal growth precisely because they have been pointing the finger at others for so long that they've never dealt with their own issues. Every time they have a falling out, they lay the fault at the other person's feet. They are then free to persist in the same patterns of negative behavior, as selfish as they've always been.

Pray that you may see more clearly from now on, to see with insight. Open your heart; allow Him to search your spirit and reveal to you those characteristics in your personality which cause problems with other people. Stop kidding yourself; sometimes it's just *you*.

Keep Your Faith

If your spirit has been injured by some insult,
shake it off and remember your reward.

Keep Your Faith

Many will mock you for believing in stories which, in their minds, rank at about the same level as fairy tales. A sea actually being parted down the middle? Water being turned to wine and blind people being healed and thousands being fed with a couple of fish and a few loaves of bread? *A dead man getting up from the grave after three days?* Surely no one would be foolish enough to actually believe such things are true! But those of us who walk by faith and not by sight know that there is a God who is able to do the impossible!

Faith is the sustaining force in the lives of God's children. It is the foundation upon which we build lives of obedience and submission to God **(Hebrews 11:1)**.

Unfortunately, it is that same faith which makes us targets of ridicule from those who don't believe. Some will scoff at you for what they see as a blind devotion to myths, and will put you down for your dedication to God and to godly things. Some secular thinkers will make you feel less than intelligent at times. They will act as though something must be wrong with you on the mental level, and will make sarcastic remarks to belittle you on the sly.

Your faith should not falter under these attacks. In fact, such assaults ought to *fortify* your faith! We would not be Christians if we did not partake in the sufferings of Christ. Jesus said, "If they persecuted me, they will persecute you also" **(John 15:20).** And He also said that *blessed* are we when they do it because we have a reward in heaven **(Matthew 5:11-12).** When the enemy attacks, don't retreat; *rejoice!*

If your spirit has been injured by some insult, shake it off and remember your reward. Pray for a renewed focus on the glory that will come from your present pain, which is evidence that God approves of you and counts you worthy of suffering for His name **(Acts 5:41).** Pray for a courageous heart to live an open and unabashed life of faith. Ask God to remove from your spirit the worry over what others think about you and replace it with a deep passion to please Him. Be steadfast and unmoving, and soon you will see what you have believed.

29

Listen Closely to Criticism

Faith is the sustaining force in the lives of God's children.

Listen Closely to Criticism

How you handle a rebuke speaks volumes about your character. We have all shot the messenger who brought us an unwelcome word. That prideful spirit within us can't stand to be corrected. As soon as it starts to feel convicted, it looks for ways to turn the tables. It compels us to lash out with personal insults, or to start looking for some flaw within *them* to expose and exploit. We hit out with hostility and aggression when others are only trying to help.

The people of Israel were good at striking out at their prophets. When men arose to rebuke their unrighteousness and to encourage them to return to the Lord, they were persecuted by the very people whom they had come to save, and some of them were even put to death.

What makes this all the more tragic is that they were not silencing men, but rather the voice of the Lord, who was trying so hard to speak truth and wisdom, to turn them away from wickedness. Stephen told the religious rulers of his day who had killed the Christ that they were just like their forefathers in their resistance of the Holy Spirit **(Acts 7:51)**. And we are no different when we harshly handle those whom God sends our way with His word!

Indeed, the truth is often *very* hard to bear. Words of warning can be heavy to your spirit when you really want what your carnal nature craves. Words of rebuke can be quite a burden when you know you are caught and convicted. And because we cannot bear them, we often try to kill the prophets who bring them. Think about how you treat those who seek to reprove and instruct you. Do you lose your temper when someone questions you? Are you quick to point out others' shortcomings when yours are brought to light? If so, you are not just rejecting the messenger, you are rejecting a gracious God who loved you enough to put that person in your path.

Pray for spiritual discernment to detect His presence in the good people He places in your life. Pray for the ears to hear His voice in the wise words of others, and ask Him to impart to you the strength of meekness and submission. When the truth hits home, do you hit back or do you humble yourself under the mighty hand of God?

Recognize and Prepare for the End

The truth is that reality is only temporary.

Recognize and Prepare for the End

The sun rises and sets every day right on time. The moon goes through its phases like clockwork, and the stars reappear in their proper places each night. The tides keep rolling in, and the rivers keep running on. The seasons come and go in the same order, year after year after year.

It's human nature to become used to the familiar things in our lives which have always been there. Because of the order and precision of nature—this magnificent machine set in motion by the Maker—we tend to become complacent in the regular routine. The more relaxed you become by the steady rhythms of the *physical* world you see every day, the less alert you will be to the unseen *spiritual* world.

II Peter 3:3-7 warns against becoming so comfortable with the constancy of creation that we lose sight of the Creator. The truth is that reality is only temporary. Take a look around you right now. Perhaps you're at home surrounded by the comforts of your life. Maybe you're on the job, and you can feel the familiar flow of the workplace. Perhaps you're sitting under the shade of a favorite tree.

Wherever you are, take a moment to say goodbye to everything you see.

Pray that the Lord will reawaken you to the reality of your eternal soul, which will outlast everything around you. Reaffirm your faith in His promise of a new heaven and a new earth **(v. 13)**, and make the daily decision to detach yourself from this old one. Put your faith and focus back on the Creator. Remember that creation, as grand and glorious as it may be, as comforting and constant as it seems, is only destined for destruction. Don't get too attached.

If you have enjoyed this book or it
has touched your life in some way,
we would love to hear from you.

Please send your comments to:
Hallmark Book Feedback
P.O. Box 419034
Mail Drop 215
Kansas City, MO 64141

Or e-mail us at:
booknotes@hallmark.com